T0294318

LITHOPEDIA

LITHO

POEMS BY ANNE KEEFE

PEDIA

BULL★CITY
PRESS

DURHAM, NORTH CAROLINA

LITHOPEDIA
Poems

Published by Bull City Press
1217 Odyssey Drive
Durham, NC, 27713
http://bullcitypress.com

Copyright © 2012 by Anne Keefe

Published in the United States of America

Library of Congress Cataloging-in-Publication Data

Keefe, Anne.
Lithopedia / Anne Keefe.
p. cm.
ISBN-13: 978-1-4243-1799-8 (Paperback)

Cover image created from images
by Claudio Arnese and Dennis Kartavenko

Book design by Flying Hand Studio

ACKNOWLEDGEMENTS

Crab Orchard Review: "If I Could Enter Your Spine as a Fish"

Cream City Review: "Fugit Amor"

The Dos Passos Review: "La voz afilla"

Eclipse: "Sylvia"

Ekphrasis: "The Orchid Whisper"

Gargoyle: "Neruda's Things"

The Grove Review: "Vespers"

The Greensboro Review: "Charm"

Harpur Palate: "Ars Poetica"

Hubbub: "Still in the Bone"

Ink Node: "The Stone Baby"

Lake Effect: "Of the Guadalquivir, Holy Week"

Potomac Review: "Puente de Triana"

Prairie Schooner: "Lemon Light"

The Southeast Review: "Most Stable Words"

Third Wednesday: "Cyclamen"

Tiger's Eye: "Qasida with Stolen Dreams"

World of Water, World of Sand: A Cape Cod Collection of Poetry, Fiction, and Memoir: "The Women Chant Words that Cross Like Tides"

CONTENTS

I

II

III

IV

V

for Delia and Frank

—

for Tyson

with many thanks to Stan Plumly

lith′əpē′dē·ən

from the Greek "lithos" meaning "stone" and "paidion"
meaning "child," and designating a fetus that has died
during an ectopic or abdominal pregnancy and turned
to bone within the body, like a sculptor turns living
flesh to stone. In this rare instance, the mother's body
protects itself from a foreign object outside of the womb.
It may remain undiagnosed for decades.

I

Deucalion cast stones behind him and thus
fashioned our tender race from the hard
marble. How comes it that nowadays, by
a reversal of things, the tender body of a
little babe has limbs nearer akin to stone?

ISRAEL SPRACH

Gynaeciorum, 1557

THE STONE BABY

In this medical fantasy the body charms
by its own devices, its tissue a myth, a village
and river lore too ancient for X-ray, too

seductive for the stiff *calcified*, the all-this-time
asymptomatic concretion. This baby is not evil
but stone-honeyed, stone-hooked, a grist and laying creature.

Always the hysteric of stability,
it is the womb that's a blinking Gorgon eye
which spies and stares the child as she flees,　　　then

spasm of floor, torso, palms open to bring out
the new thing, throat against the cries

that do not come. Your fatted heels and fists
dig and choke, dig and wallow in muscle.　　　Dig,

dig and subside.
　　　　　　　　Soon, you are a fine etching,
a thin harmony to mother's own marrow.

The century ages and you feel a memory,
lithiasis of the still pelvis. A slate for wounds
fixed there in the dancing belly.　　　If you will sleep,

my lithopedion, sleep. Little stone-cricket,
stone-fox, stone orpine and pippin,
my uprooted fossil, lily snapped from stalk.

LITHOGRAPH

The line of her neck to shoulder then hand
to stone moves like breathing moves
through her into the white rock, the waxy line settling.

We've talked about the title, Protection,
the loosed birthing from egg and pod.
The protectors, the protected, treasures

of nature that sunned on kitchen patios:
two perfect siliquae, seed husk, locust
that caught a certain light, sketched,

drawn to the pale smooth of limestone, inked
and pressed, inked, and the paper—layer
upon layer printed, pressed to make the whole.

In the final print, still in the air, three leaves
are vertically suspended, caught in the web
of a spider bent on ordering chaos

like alphabetizing the unborn. Is it that
the protectors have failed, they lie cast-off,
useless—no, used, remnants of selves,

stones my mother will save, piled in a closet,
stone upon stone like children's graves.
Hatched, I'm the wind-egg, nothing will root.

IF I COULD ENTER YOUR SPINE AS A FISH

One night, with each thumbtip
in the well on either side of the bone,
I split the skin at the base and swim.
My once-lungs sift strange particles,
salts of carbonate and phosphate of lime,
where desire accumulates, like acid.
The current is thick. Up over the rocky
fissures, I learn to move in the new form.
I curve the roped ligaments of neck
carried by the flux until I wedge myself
between the stone marrow and thin skin
of your chest. Tight, you feel the pulse
of my breathing, gills and flutter of scales,
their knife-edges drawn along the grain.
I am still. You move as if by instinct
or a memory to cover the spot where
I bulge from your collarbone. You feel
the beat under your hand as a heart.
Your fingers define the edges
of fish body, search the skin, widening
crevices toward the web of fin,
the white curve of underbelly.
For a moment, it seems you might
push me deeper, unhook me from the crag
and send me fluent to the core. But
you open the flesh with your hands,
flush rising to your cheeks as you take me
from you, hold me to light between finger
and thumb, silver fish of dreams,
red, gasping against the foreign air.

LITHOPEDIA : RADIATION CASE REPORT

The first is debatable, either
1100 BC or 3100 years untouched
in the spine of History's stock footage.

These children make a wonder in the body's
own clay, twice fossilized and thought
the rarest constellation of severe defect.

To imagine it, the dust unveils a mummified
curl of parchment stone, cradled like a pearl
in oyster flesh, unearthing of a century's long lying in.

Yet, today's electromagnetic eye makes a phantom
of the tiny bird's ribs, the abstract skeleton
a bowl of skull and tucked tailbone, the

ghost baby clasping feet and hands in
prayer or frozen in a nightmare spell,
a soft thing turned to stone.

CHARM READER

You must pay in trinkets of spring,
for she has the insatiable heart
of a child and sees blankly
the thing inside you do not recognize.

Haul out your history from the heavy bottom drawer:
your own book safe in its cellophane,
the two-inch footprint on slick paper, the oval
box, delicate, bowed.

The key inside will fortify.
It will be your talisman, your amulet
among so many. The charm reader
does not read death poems.

She chants to crows at rush hour.
She picks out your voice, starts
at your number in the din. You see only
that your coming here was fated.

Blind, bewitched, charm-struck baby.
The key mixes with sweat in your fist—
open it, now, to crocus bone of a bulb,
a tiny onion in your hand.

STILL IN THE BONE

I don't remember but they tell me
that somehow my body knew the music
as its own. I'll picture the church later
but my dancing that day is a dream,
another life lived outside of time, a vapor
lying down like a wafer on my tongue and
smoke of new speech as a birth within my teeth.
I'm aware of my voice, which is not mine.
The people understand and are impressed,
they smile as they do when a child moves
by raw instinct. When I wake, the dance
is an ancient language still in the bone.
Even now, in a moment, or a certain turn,
I feel it sigh in its sleep.

LINES ON A FAVORITE THEME

You should know, I like to write
about being alone. Not alone-alone,
alone with someone. I'll do it with you
if you let me, or even if you don't.

You'll have to understand that
I cherish it, the isolation, indulgent
meditation on, say, each evenly-
spaced button of the duvet.

No, really, I see past it all, watch it
blur with paced breath out of the body,
and mine, in and out of yours,
a universe moving in soft bursts.

While you sleep, I can be angry
with you for not sharing the world
that opens to me in the night.
I won't be happy, though, not until

I've heaved and sighed enough
to wake you, pull you above me,
building the cage of your arms
and chest around myself.

That's when I'll claw at you,
drawing out what I love most,
some wolf-eye that glints in you.
I want it in me. I want to be

small and soft in a darkness
bigger than both of us. So dark,
I won't see your mouth, but will lift
myself to it, already tasting the bite.

THE SECOND WIFE OF LIR

> She drove the children of Lir into the lake to bathe ... and put them
> into the forms of four beautiful, perfectly white swans....
>
> — W. B. YEATS, *Irish Fairy and Folk Tales*

In the poem, I wanted to become her.
I liked her two faces, sister-in-law and new wife.

I liked the dark pleasure of the husband
knowing the two as one, both his wives
together in dreams. Imagine how I'd lie with him,

wanting him to want me. I know it's sick,
but knowing me, it'd be just enough

to let me curse a sister's memory.
Each night, I'd watch his dream-born eyes
open themselves, that royal chin hanging

and the jaw line just a slant of air, predawn.
I'd know it before waking to it, haunting

the room like a ghost. Maybe the first night
I'd search, innocent bride, eyes wide
to how he marks the bend of day,

frame to the fire like a witch at her spells.
Once would be enough. Him lighting the girl's face

and painting mother onto daughter's skin—
don't think it would take me long to realize
he'll only ever know me with his hands.

And each day, with full sun, he'd be gone,
hiding among furze and the false dark of earth.

Eventually, I'd be jealous enough to do it
(it's my witchiness here that's appealing),
eventually, I would take my sister's children to bathe,

three boys ahead and the daughter's hand
in my own. She and I would speak names

of flowers together, singing together like two girls
before the afternoon: wood sorrel, trefoil, black meddick.
Only I know the words have meaning.

That morning, in the lake, reflections would lift
and play like the feathers of swans.

How I'd listen to them change—the children's voices,
human and not human. They'll never grow
old. Swans measure their years in lakes.

Lir will see me, later in the story and aged like himself:
my changed skin, my crooked voice.

THE ORCHID WHISPER

for Tyson

When we linger
in MOMA to catch
Kentridge's clockwork puppet

in its mechanical dance—
a tin butterfly hunching
wings again in a sprung arch—

I see, also, the flat-faced
phalaenopsis, the moth orchid
you tend so faithfully.

I love the small patterns
about you: a well-made thumb
wiping the drop of water

from pot's rim, the quiet way
you press into my palm,
keen work of your language

in my ear. I know, too,
how you kiss blush into each petal
too delicate for skin.

You are a red moon orchid.
A squirrel-footed thelymitra, jewel-
tongued ghost and spinach

blue. You are the root and song
of my life, hummed precision,
a balance in which I cradle.

LULLABY

You have only to part lips,
you alarmed, and the birds squandering,
toothless and wingèd, into a caged air.

I imagine (don't look at me so) I can't hear, just switch
and tock of each dove marking space:
this is my life, and that, yours.

No doubt you've known all along.
You, with your geometrical heart, measuring
the new cry along the width of your forearm.

And me, I've had my time with you, your sweat
too sweet, and still, always, your spine
whispering like the edge of the sea to sky.

I don't begrudge you your second desire. I, too,
want to hold the infant organ as it beats.
I, too, want the thyme, the cinnamon warmth

as it strums through the belly, cello, mandolin.
You could rock the sea to its final sleep.
I watch the angles rise, alarmed, birds.

II

Those fragile things—
they fill harbors
and markets with light,
wild gold, and we open
two halves of a miracle.

PABLO NERUDA
"Oda al Limón"

LA VOZ AFILLA

The new pills vivify my dreams,
body close to the water's surface,

breathing air and the liquid like two beings.
It's all of it raw, the splitting of flamenco

voice, seguiriya, la voz afilla, broken
in two. Virgins can't sing cante jondo.

So, this year I will be made virgin again
to learn again the cutting open,

dark space where song comes from
and where I hide what feels like love.

It's the history they hold, gypsy soleares
like a Lorca dove in the dark palm,

a tiny white capsule I swallow before sleep.
When the voice returns it will tell of two bodies

but this time as myth, the tale made skin
against skin, soft tongue and the pagan throat.

A safe distance from which to sing again,
to swallow memory. I will choke on my own

voice, on the water welling at nostril and breast.
To choke meaning. Choke out the song.

VESPERS

Abbazia di Sant'Antimo

Sound has moved like this before.
The monastery, a tooth in the green night,
and the noiseless stones gathering close.
Stones cut themselves to smaller stones
until they sound inside. White is soft
and cold as a palm to the breastbone.
As if from underneath folded hands,
this light might expose the failure
of the flushed body. A cherished wound—
some thing you remember believing in
but don't now or won't say. The monks enter
parallel like ten ribs. Their voice increases
and divides ten times. You stop. It will
breathe for you, pale ceiling, a body's lung.

LITHOPEDION FROM THE CASE FILE OF DR. WILLIAM H. H. PARKHURST, 1853

A found poem

the mother one widow Mrs. Amos Eddy age 77
the full 46 years child
most astounding freak of nature

the hero physician
of graveyard autopsy
preparing a boiled dinner

entirely ossified
kettle upset forcibly into
the little fixings ready for use

and the wished for never came
he turned his horse again to pasture
never to be revealed

except by knife
almost floating in the abdomen
resting on the symphasis publis its face

toward cartilaginous structure
thighs flexed upon body legs
flexed upon thighs

hence the forearm and hand
offered to the hard and irregular surface
the mother's spine

PUENTE DE TRIANA

Every few years a new bridge rises
out of the dirty river like the spine
of a prostitute. Isabel II is the seventh,
counting left to right. It's pretty

recent, though apparently they were going
for that antique look—the sophistication
inherent in old lampposts, metal workings,
and the great masses of pocked rock

like a thousand small half moons. On Saturdays,
highschoolers try climbing the sides,
little awkward animals, and perhaps one loses
a shoe and it falls to the gravel bank.

Clearly, you see the bridge. We've just
walked across it, sharing a glance
at the uneasiness of its sigh beneath traffic,
and now you see it because you follow the line of my finger through the air—

you cannot not see it. Still there's all
the construction: metal, tar, cranes
growing into the mesh of sky. I point
to Spain, not mine but even more not yours, and—.

An ant has crawled on your leg.
The cranes line themselves parallel
to the river, laid flat against the air.
The lamps are golden mosquitoes in the sultry

Sevilla dusk. Fact is, we're just tourists
and the bridge, it isn't old but simply
the work of hands. A woman, Isabel
the second or seventh, most feminine, most

graceful. I like wondering if it's machismo to use her,
to travel her curves as we travel the stroke

of brush on canvas. Like living in the idea of great art,
I've walked her false borders these months here.

She's a bridge of people. You felt her move.

OF THE GUADALQUIVIR, HOLY WEEK

There at the edges of cross-hatched leaves
the air is thick in the gray-toned palms, weighted
and bending around the body like a thousand waxy fingertips.
The fish jump in this river.

On the opposite bank, Triana's wind lifts
the draped mesh hung to catch remnants. Perhaps it could
lessen the intensity to remove all those tiles, could free
la viuda from her lace-screened street watching.

I imagine the widow at her balcony now.
She has been resting with onion-stained hands
curled to her breast. She's made a stew
flavored with whole skeletons of fish.

She has lost four sons and now she dreams of them,
sees them grown: drinking, laughing, beating
time in their palms. They wear the palms of men.
She sees the eldest pressing the body of a woman

against the bricks of the apartment. She watches it all
as if from her window: how her son's hand trickles down
a woman's belly, how the earth layers with wax,
the thousand candles of semana santa. Soon, the streets will crowd

for the virgin. She'll float on the backs of thirty men,
wearing their necks raw. A woman with her head back will
not open her eyes. The bricks press into her skin. It's dusk.
Her palms spread against the made wall.

LEMON LIGHT

JOSEPH BEUYS, *Capri-Batterie*, 1985

At the Boston MFA there's a strange lemon
with a plug and light-bulb attached. It rests on its side,
so that the bulb's bulb and the lemon's bulb
form a cartoonish 'L' inside the glass museum cube.

At the time, we talked about what makes art and laughed
and now I'm angry with myself for noticing only
how the dimpled rind swelled around the metal,
the yellow-to-green-to-blue mold and crust crawling up

each prong into the black socket. Because,
as it turns out, there was a whole philosophy
inside that lemon. The acid working as a galvanic battery
that could bring to light a new world in 60 watt doses.

Inside that lemon, inside the delicate honeycomb
of the multitude, was infinite translucent energy,
living in pulp, the cells holding force like spaces between
nerves of an insect's wing. Like a net for the acid's heat.

And wasn't it warmth that he wanted, lying there
in La Certosa, his lungs failing him and beauty
failing him. What can the body do but lose its charge,
as it rests in the sun, coming up with ways to make us smile.

MOST STABLE WORDS

Year might mean *old* or *worn out*
says the linguist, and I know you
and I are scared by that. We're silent
in the implicit naming of the end.
Who knows, the body, it might be full
of sun music, dripping over a horn lip,
salt on a slick palm, delicate, weightless.
Then slowly, the heart's eye might stop
looking to the moon of the nail,
each knuckle fading away from the hand.
If it will die one long night into dawn,
then it will. We'll know, two eyes
too worn to the other's. We'll see it,
and not. And know. The new year.

NERUDA'S THINGS

three great loves
three wives
three houses

1. La Chascona—

crouches in the cliffsides like a man
in a small boat, neck bent, arms out
as awkward wings to hold the body steady.
He'll always crouch like this, remembering
coming upon her as she slept, Matilde,
her hair a fire he has dreamed himself
inside so many nights. Tasted la rosada
in his mouth, familiar wine from tinted glass.
He curves around tree trunks like a vine,
a telephone cord bringing the world
inside and unwanted, like things, sea
treasures worn with sand and ropes made
thick and solid as bone by men's hands.

2. La Sebastiana—

holds a horse inside. Tied up, it'll
never breathe the whirling wind through
its painted nostrils. Never rise up or fall
with the slim girl's legs molding to the wooden
mane. Her laugh is a high and eerie calliope.
Only the smoke will rise, its bulk almost
solid, rising in a hurricane glass
bigger than a man, taller, because upstairs
the room is just a cage. He sat on a cloud here,

collecting what couldn't be contained. Even
now, his chair still stained with the green
ink of a favorite pen. Night sky over the water,
singing its loneliness in the wet, salty fog.

3. Isla Negra—

was always his favorite. Rows on rows
of miniatures: ships in bottles, six thousand
shells, butterflies and butterflies and
all the tiny worlds enclosed in glass, ready to toss
out to sea. They say he looked a la vidrio
and saw a ship's hatch floating in on the Pacific.
It became his desk. Finally, he had to bring Medusa in,
too many locals praying at her like the Virgin.
They say her glass eyes cry in winter. Nina.
Pinta. Santa Mar—why does a man need all three?
Why always the sea and women, the looking
out over the water, while in his house
the greatest love waits like a new life.

GINSBERG,

When you say, in the long, chugging
lines of your Greyhound poem, how
you built yourself up—arms pumping
the bags high overhead into that massed grid
of baggage racks, skeleton about the organs
of our silly possessions, going this way or
that, even our bodies becoming innards
just covered by a bus's skin,
by the air of the terminal—when you say,
to end the poem, when you name the muscles
pectoral, when you make them *big as vagina*,
I can't read, anymore, my own sex, reading you
unfold the folded web onto your breast,
feeling the muscle tighten at the word not said.

DREAM OF TWO CATS

I'm searching
for a picture
of us.

It wouldn't exist, though
I see it, framed,
the underside of your arm

and its paleness across my belly.
Somehow, I'm mother
to a son

I don't know.
His small, perfect body
from my own.

I have lost and am losing him.
Perhaps by drowning.
His roundness,

nectarine:
a moon I saw once.
A little shack

on a floating lawn.
One vicious cat.
You've left me.

The land breaks apart
to water like
a son returning:

a second cat.
Within the room,
a mother knows her own.

One sleek cat body
lures the next,
combining like women

in a movie I saw:
as through cotton,
a familiar curve of vein.

ISLA NEGRA

for P. N.

And now I've seen it, your own air,
the naked stone and how it takes the water,
a body both jagged and warm.

Here you lie calmly buried
in the two faces of a lover,
a fiery profile that you must repeat, tracing

the edges as mountains and valleys
in the gold lazy sand.
I hear her name as it splinters in the spray.

I see the lance of old pearl, a magical horn
that rents the oyster. I see the sea
opened to you on your own shore.

Poet, how you tried to contain it,
searching the tinted glass for the cool bell
that would finally hold,

oh, how you tried to grow the day
like a single flower
as the light changed its skin ever to shade.

III

Mother, the moon is dancing
in the courtyard of the dead.

FEDERICO GARCÍA LORCA
"Danza de la lúa en Santiago"

QASIDA WITH STOLEN DREAMS

after FEDERICO GARCÍA LORCA, *Diván del Tamarit*

I. Of the body returning to itself

Like drowning upward into the Massachusetts sky,
the woman allows stones to line her skin,
shaded, half cool, half warm.

They are the thousand windows
at a thousand terraces that hold back water
from the small hands of children.

There's something at her feet. She knows
its pain before her foot moves toward—
as if she remembers the sting. She's not

surprised by the bitter root at her arch.
The bitter inside her face.
Night heals itself after birth.

II. Of the reborn

In this town a child dies every afternoon.
An old woman pats her empty belly and announces
her pregnancy: claims seven young inside.

At 63, a dried womb, never so full as in death.
She lay there three days. The family goes back,
sorts through her things, and looking

at the spot, they imagine it was like the body
underwater. The mind a dying star, and how
it all makes them so uncomfortable, how

once, in a grocery store I saw a woman
with her shirt stuffed, the buttons straining
to hold it—a pillow? She hummed

as she fingered the tiny jars of baby food.
My mother said: she must have lost one.
It's true that children wear the dark wings of moss.

III. Of the younger son

He's died so many times that
the memory becomes worn, a blanket covering
the grandmother's knees that she recognizes now,

and now. And now she weeps, caught
in the wall between dream and death,
the living tulip and the sickly.

In my only memory, my uncle's arms circle
a tree while mine reach not even halfway.
My cheek and stomach pressed to the bark,

I feel the ridges grown deep.
Soon the new-leaf green, bright, like a mantis,
and the memory wooden to my breast.

IV. Of the once delicate waist

No one understood her perfume,
the dark magnolia of her belly, though
the family loves to imagine her: just 98 pounds

at her wedding, so slender no shoe fit
her foot. I carry the blood of her
veins. In my mouth the light for her death.

In her coffin, her hands will be too swollen
and her lips, thin enough that I see the teeth
in the skull, under the skin, under their stitching.

I don't want to hear how the dead are still
thirsting. I want to sleep, only don't mistake me
for that. I'm trapped somehow in white

and black, looking into the open
earth, forgetting to breathe or swallow.
I decide to watch myself from above. I watch

my body bend to the stone. I want to touch
the virgin's face and feel my hand atop her,
crossing my thumb on the marble like Ash

Wednesday in Catholic school, always
that crooked thumb smearing gray.
There's music but everything heard as if through water.

V. Of the sound of weeping

I've closed the window. I don't want to hear
the weeping. Out there, there's nothing but
sound, a wall around time: before my birth,

after. The grandmother stares at me till I realize
I'm a stranger staring at her.
My father translates her mind's device, then—

the sob of her memory, a sound like one I hear
behind me one day in a restaurant.
A low, pained sigh, real whales on a record

I played as a child. In the restaurant, I turn
to find that it's a deaf girl, laughing.
I can barely hold the weeping in my hand.

VI. Of the older son

My father's alone, a city asleep
in his throat. His voice, it will be so soft,
like his hand over her hair. I saw it

in an old filmstrip of my parents' wedding,
how my grandmother hugged him and she couldn't let go—
everything was still—and I saw just how

he bent to her, whispering something
that must have sounded like prayer.
The son and his agony, face to face.

In one sad instant, he'll hint at the grief
over coffee, he'll say: it's a strange thing,
being alive in the world without either parent.

VII. Of the woman becoming

The night is like bad silver. The sand
is cool and fine along my back,
the itch and shiver of skin, not for a lover,

but because I can't see his face,
because the night is cold and thick
and this landscape so raw, I can't be

certain that there aren't animals here.
I don't remember the fire but I smell
the pit out of which the ashes catch

the clear wind and rise. One breath
and I'm again in those few seconds
of confession, willing to hollow myself.

There's something, cramped metal
hanging and stiff—the girl of tears
bathing in flames. Burned wings.

A blindness filming over the eyes
like warped lighthouse glass.
If I move too much, I will fall.

VIII. Of the (grand)mother

The one was the other and the woman remaining
was neither. She asks: where is my tomb?
But there's just silence, thick, moist-dry

like the host to her tongue. She's song-tide,
moving up the nave, past each pew.
The sound is only her own. It fills,

touches the walls and the church becomes
her body, the bone pillars, and a muscle,
walled to breathing—

somewhere are people, being. Where
is my tomb? They wonder
at those whom they know as myth.

When I dream, all worlds end in this one,
in fall at once cold and warm,
the breathing rhythmic and stopped.

In the room my mouth catches
in red, the woman watches, our
bodies open to place words at the altar.

IV

A model may suggest, or awaken and bring
to a conclusion, by a movement or position,
a composition that lies dormant in the mind.

AUGUSTE RODIN

FUGIT AMOR

Bronze, c. 1884

In Seville, Rodin's room was hastily built,
a room within a room: the museum walls
all enormous oils and the sculptures

huddled at the center, each an egg in its carton.
In the afternoons, I walked the maze
of partitions, looking to catch the two alone.

I brought you here once. I dragged you
through thick air, right to the two of them,
Francesca and Paolo, arching birds' wings.

You didn't really see them—only their bodies,
enough nudity to make your lip curl, aroused
at Francesca's pain burst open before you.

I wanted to cover her breasts with my own—
feeling time and your interest in my new skin,
reduced to a movement, a spine lithe in the air.

They make a twin sail. They never touch.
Only tears in the wind's current travel one face
to the other. Each can taste the other.

Meanwhile, you circled the stone, catching the pair
from every angle. They form an axis,
fury of scent and noise. A star's wind. Like

when I finally left you and I heard myself scream.
You cried. Which made me hate you. And
you didn't catch my shoulders in your hands,

didn't turn my face toward yours. Mine was a howl,
distinct, horrible. It opened and opened again until
it was its own body of air—a lover from my throat.

ARS POETICA

I can't write about the Russian crack
whore because what would I know
and because, you'll laugh, I only
saw her tonight, some girl in a movie.

It's just that when she's cleaned up,
dressed, and her back's exposed
under black silk, I remember again
how young she is. Her muscles cover

over her bones with the heaviest gray—
an artist's gum holding her body
and the room, lifting mistakes
as she climbs a thousand stairs.

In the garish shot, a casino scene,
it's all I see, her skin: slender bulk
and sinew then, underneath it and
spiraling—memory not quite erased.

TO CLAIM THE BODY —

I'll have to finally ask it of myself,
grasping the linen, lifting to peek

at the slack form, the body
formerly known.

Why those sighs of desire for the sheer thrall?
It had never been real.

I'd find out—this many years, that many
later—my body has only been memory.

No trick and tickle fingertips
along the belly. No nipple-pinch, goose

pimple breathlessness for something
harder and something—

I've made it too difficult.
I've over-thought the consequences.

See, here, these lines mark borders,
outline, identifying scars. Stars

constellated in the world's time.
I trace a foreign name along this skin,

try to remember a history washing
to white on the page. These words

make definite grief of loss I never had.
I have only seen women die.

THE POEM THAT
NAMES ITSELF

                          stands before me
the figure of confidence. He knows how I love
lying with him, lifting to his face, pointing my toes

to his calves under warm sheets. He suspects
that I've even let myself think he's perfect.

But the poem itself is odd, bodiless,
strange. A whispered thing, an almost—.

I know its charm to the tongue like an old master.

I know hands that reach to open the book, pressing
pages flat to break the binding. Pressing the hands

flat against breasts, pressing down to cover with cloth.
Making a way around me, skin brushing my side
ducking under an arm, pulling close and smooth.

He works his task well. Down, over hips,
smoothing, humming. The page is a bright white.

Inside it I am hot. The hot hot white, inside the cocoon
and, hallucinating, my skin becomes the page.

The fibers harden to stone. I lose my only, only my

poem that names itself cracks
open like a wind-egg offering shadows.

Meant to hold more than these slim particles, yet
somehow, a sudden coming upon nothing:

lack covered over, a woven shell
protecting history inside the bowled world.
I want to know its stories, to build its

memory house with wood and stone. Standing
at each window, wiping the glass clean, I feel grit

between my fingers. I see, maybe,
dishes near a stove, some broken, and a bird inside,
bathing itself in a dusty corner.

Of course, it would look like I need it to look, like
some token of experience I feel—like shape

in the poem, how it comes, inverted,
to a kind of being, how a cast opens to reveal
the form in solid air. I dip my hands

along the wells for breast and stomach,
and the shell's inner wall is smooth as skin

or paper. I want to be close. To smell it—
smell the taste in my mouth like a past life.

MADAME CHATRI'S STONE BABY —

is a true lithopedion, a star unborn in the best-selling autopsy findings
of 1582 and then sold to the Museum of Curiosities, Paris, where the
eyes of the young balk at the little haunted mummy, all crab and snipe
in its shelled display, a spectacle which might be a bit of a shame after
the 28 years that Madame carried it, but then it seems that a sculpted
child can live indefinitely and so it is bought and sold and sold and
bought, until the King of Denmark places it in his royal Museum in 1653,
and then, 200 years later, the baby, like the other Danish treasures,
ends up in the Museum of Natural History and then, some time after
that, the object, the baby, is lost, or stolen, forgotten or perhaps buried,
because it is an oddity and because, by then, it is very much out of style.

BALZAC

Nude Study, 1892–93, *Bronze*

You are Rodin's Balzac. You are the muscle
and gut of a king, standing there after sex
with the weight of bronze on your left heel.
I'm surprised you're not embarrassed
after your sumptuous meals and that dexterous
hand at the wine. Your belly of decadence.
But you're so proud the fat of your stomach
becomes real metal, a sculpture where even
your limp penis seems bigger. Standing there,
you appear the essence of man. And even though
I don't love you, I envy your majesty
modeled in the middle of an awkward bedroom,
a picturesque mistake of flesh. In a moment where
I would mask my shame, you stand up into art.

BODY LANGUAGE

We learn it early here, a first taste
of our own tongues, a word

rich and solid in the mouth,
frothed and buttery to taste.

I know the word in every tongue.
I catch, even, furtive caresses in a crowd.

Here, the French giggling in their cigarette pants,
and here, a Spaniard who wants only to touch my hair.

Here, too, amid the Scottish cream,
the word is drunk and stocky. But, like you

I am a figure of three dimensions.
I know the word like a moon of porcelain,

an oath, a god's limbs held between the teeth.
I know retort, bodice, the structure versus the soul.

Oh yes, I cast a shadow, the bone, the hull,
the bulk of anything, even

the foundation of your silk hat. I know it.
The word makes its skin over me.

So they tell me.
Tallow melts in the word's own heat.

Here, as it happens, I can't tell
if I will spoil, rot in process, but

there is the resonance, the vertebra on vertebra fitted
to hold and receive. The word is

an agent of phenomena. Among glassware
and crisp linen, the word cleans its plate.

BONNARD'S GIRL

All morning, it's like I've caught her in corners,
peek-a-boo, her eyes blue or sometimes not.
She's a child just jumped in the frame, coy,
waiting for me to see her. Or she looks down,
demure and warm, but her cheek and jaw always
with that same curve, the nose and lips of a doll.

Even nude in the bath, she's so small, though
the body is a woman's—maybe not the only
but the one he knew well, the skin with a texture
like his hand there in the water with her. He painted
the tub to follow her hip and breast, so that the room
is her body, tones of paint and muscle built like home.

———————

But then, in the photographs, I'm shocked
by her colorless form: Marthe removing
her night dress. Marthe seated, Marthe
seated with her left hand behind her neck,
Marthe seated with her hand on her right breast
in the garden at Montval. In the garden

at Montval, Marthe crouching down, Marthe
bending to touch the ground, Marthe holding
her night dress—I'm in love with her—
Marthe in the sunlight, Marthe in the real,
so much more, I think I could have touched her,
felt hips between my hands, full as my own.

FIGURE OF SAPPHO

> Though it isn't easy for us to rival
> goddesses in the loveliness of their figures [
>
> — SAPPHO, *trans. Jim Powell*

Her ease never questioned.

We see her always as statue,

        sculpted body [   ] the mythic

dust of its island. O come [

      ] rose-armed girl
      ] that kind of lover
      ]

                  [goddess]
gathering her women to the altar.

Of course they would have born their breasts.
          ] *women once danced this way* [
          ]

They would have circled, drinking

wine that trickled the skin
      weak blood in the sand.

The loveliness of the figure,
    [pure]
               here [   ]
                  [cast]   in bronze

here
carved beneath gauzed
folds of marble

       [   ]
       [   ]
coupling here

    with those slim girls of the canvas [

[   ] so she said,
      ] *O Dream on your dark wings*

no rival, indeed, to the voice's   [form]

     as it falls
        [   ]
           to time,
                reaching [

] *keep off the cruel* [

     without the expectation of touch,

    ] *don't you remember*

      opening a live heart to air

[moon]

GLOSA WITH REFRAIN FROM LORCA

When the moon appears
in its same hundred faces,
the silver coin
weeps in the pocket.

I catch a strange eye in anything:
a window, spoon, another eye.
When mirrors stop reflecting
I start to stare. And when the moon appears

there are two men: you in real time
and the one who exists in dreams.
Both of you blur into the hollow,
the same hundred faces pitted close to my pelvic bone.

The one, he stretches himself taut
along my thigh. I feel each breath, each beat
burying his pointed face further. His chin
takes on heat like a silver coin at my neck.

When the moon appears, when my eyes
meet my own eyes, I'll know it for sure:
I knew then what I know now. With you,
memory weeps in the pocket.

TO THE MUSE

Camille Claudel, 1864–1943

I've no right to be angry writing this poem
to you, Camille, though I want to ask the pointed questions:

How it was your first time
with him—did you play it coy? Did you say:

Master Rodin, how will you have me?
And did he speak, meet your eyes or only

mold your body, hand to waist, darling Camille
like a clay figurine. I'll say, too coldly, that

between sculptors language is all touch.
I want to imagine it this way:

he taught you what he learned at Petite École,
drawing the shape in the air, eyes closed

so that dimensions of the other take the mind's form.
Figure outlined becoming an extension of fingertips.

Who draped the backdrop that allowed
him to circle and circle to set the edges in stone?

Of course, this is what I see, bearded sorcerer-god,
did you feel him turn your skin cold—

                              you, a virgin
at the studio's center. I'll ask: was the sex like sacrifice?

Because, now, among all the Dante, the Hugo and Balzac,
we can barely track how often bronze catches your shadow.

The nudes repeat your arches, the spine, lip,
ear, navel, thigh. These are borders

of feminine against the rock. Woman,
an egg in the massive hand.

What of your own work? Camille, forgive me,
I assume he did not understand. I assume the pupil kneels

too easily, begging, as she does in your own L'age Mûr.
Would we find you on your knees if he hadn't

returned to his angel? You know they ask it:
would we find you at all?

V

Day now, night now, at head, side, feet,
They stand their vigil in gowns of stone....

SYLVIA PLATH

"The Disquieting Muses"

MEDUSA RUBENESQUE

Just the head, not the folds
and layers of fleshy succulence
nor the thighs beneath the fur twisted
so as to belong to another loved body.

No, only the decapitated thing,
hooded with its many snakes
and those wormed reptilian entrails
ribboning off from the neck's hollow.

Man-trap bitch and beauty—
how quickly your face sallows
and your smart temples gray
at the border of skin and scale.

How even your dead Gorgon eye
fixes the mere glance. This painter
of bodies, then, stills your horror
in the lacking form—the womb that births

a flying horse from its throat. Bosom,
hip, the sculpted kneecap, the cold
arching foot.

No, charmer, spectacle,
your own locks bite and hiss. Your lips
open, green and chapped with venom.

CHARM

I call forth a poison of change,
    I chant the ripe body and place
        a thumb to taut skin.

The fleshy meal full in palm
    and godless words—slick, red—
        I call: By my hands

let me be bound, the pulp
    bound under the winding,
        form to rot and become again.

By my hips let me be bound.
    Belly, breasts, the winding
        sheet, let it bind. The atoms

remake themselves by cells' spell.
    A mirrored coffin to hold the girl, to wake
        the kiss. By my lips let it bind.

By my voice let there be no longer
    a god, only words and the body,
        let there be the flesh, thumbtip bruised

and seam-split. Let the golden scissors cut.
    By my eyes let me see myself not
        myself. By my eyes, so mote it be.

THE STONE GARDEN

Even gods make a monster of the victim,
and here I am, no exception, stranded,
the changing sand a fixed surface of desire.

Don't get me wrong, I've still got it.
The suitors creep up my shore
regular as moon tide, plumed in their best

helmets, their armor shining fractals
of dragon scales and thin as tin to my glance.
As a girl, they could barely hide their want.

They gulped hunger at Athena's altar for me,
for my other body: lithe priestess
supple and golden beneath white robes,

the hair tamed and plaited with oil,
the feet twined in soft leather. Now, I crave
even a rough palm around each aching tusk—

I thirst for the tongue to my withered lip,
the embrace to contain this body's grotesque
wilderness—now I would welcome the ravishing.

Instead, each hero grows my garden by one.
I make them my own. Their features reveal too
much the horror of what I have become

and so, with stone and dull-weighted blunt,
I soften the terror that froze them from within.
The limestone is pliant enough that I work it

easily, clawing at eyes and face until
the stone skin cracks and withers. I teach
my still young warriors the monstrous rhythm

of this island. I hear the wind hiss
about me, knowing always that the end
will come on feathered breeze, silent,

simple as seeing my mirrored own.

LITHOPEDIA : THE CASE
OF THE VANISHING TWIN

calcification
is the true test of bondage
between you and me

a minute's frenzied
outburst then stone arms circle
your living throat's wail

MATERNAL CARESS

MARY CASSATT, *Oil on canvas*, 1896

She's not even beautiful,
this ruddy, cherub-cheeked child
with her head tilted back as

she looks down her little nose
and sees this other body as her own.

Mama won't be her first word
because we need not name
the thing that is the source, the wake

and sleep of our small world
that raises the sun and shades the shy skin.

Oh we know the heart's beat
between the breasts as our own breath.
We grab at the mirrored face (the caress

here is no pet) and test our young legs
against abdomen, knowing, always,

the arm that holds like a wave's face,
palm, the fingertips' skin against skin.

This is the first language. A mother
and her own, a struggling pink moon

against the gray. How we know its
patient blue eye, its hungry cry.

TWO WOMEN

take
the same fall

only one
chooses it

the first almost
a girl still

laughing
with her boyfriend

at the top
of a mall

how does
she slip

over the
escalator

rail
does she

scream
does she

know it
as it

happens
does she

bargain
with her god

while
the other

woman
circles

the rim
of a college

stadium
plans her

flight as she
gains

momentum
takes her

swift
action

        making
        good
her
promise

        even
        as she
gives up
the message

        the body
        leaves
below
a swollen

        testament
        of how
much
a gift

        to
        soar
really
costs

        for us
        to
think it
we must

        feel
        the whir
like
a bird's

        heart
        within
the paper
ribs

SYLVIA,

They say Sexton felt betrayed
when you did it and it stuck.

In her poem, the two of you court
the same boy, little teenage death who's

for one a lover, the other a son.
Of course you know Ted's dead.

So now there's a movie, a girl
playing at you. I don't have to tell you how

the audience can't understand
the soft bread as it tears under the butter, milk,

a tray, their tiny bedroom—listen,
I know. Just like—

these people, they don't get that
poet and mother are different bodies.

That somehow the topic just comes up
over martinis and sad pills, the dark fantasy.

That even young, sexy, we fear
our own wombs, dizzy swimming folds,

knotted cells and the blood that would drown
ten delicate fingers, ten translucent toes.

We need nine lives. We need the house
on Mercy Street and we need its basement,

that crevice within the cement
where this body fits and that body survives.

CYCLAMEN

After H. D.

I've never written a poem about you
and you are not a god,
but I ask your long flank
to lie beside me.

I ask your curls and
your dark look to be remade
for the light of a face
to face my own.

I ask, even, for the mask
(the one you made so famous)
because it is easier to pray
to the myth of you.

———————

These things are more than
easy for you. The mask
is no blasphemy and your thigh
doubles simply with mine

still, the root with which you hold
tight within the mud,
the spearheaded reach of your tongue
licks smooth the tearful petal.

———————

I thought the petal would wither
with the salt of touch.

I thought—I think, no one
could want it.

Like the lush-hued fruit
dries in the sun, the dense
speck of flower
not petal, not sun,

not the berry mouth and
crevice of the lip against lip,
not the tongue, little flake
of red snow.

———————

This time, I will be the cyclamen
and you will pluck
rusted petals from a golden stem.
The fire you promise

makes no difference
to the taste in your mouth.
Will you fall to the sea-fall
of cyclamen? The wine,

the grapes you do not savor,
the thick petal red
a metallic flesh inside you,
always ripe and ripening.

PETITION

Take something from me, idle
and mad as I am both. Take
idle and the low beat of breath,
a song whisped so I cannot hear.

Give up worship and take. Take
hot, take mad illusion, dark mood,
the frenzied reddening skin, the blood-
drummed ear. I am winning.

I feel I am winning while you are caught
in the dance. For now, the dance refuses,
music always plays its own hand.
Still, we up the score.

We pray too hard. Mere sweet
addiction, this, a seduction
too simple for the mechanism of philosophy
that drives you to your dreams.

I lie awake. I feel you are letting me win.
How long will you ignore
the game already begun? Compete, love,
you must come to realize

I live in a soul birthed in solitude.
Instinct will always play. The soft body,
the caress—these things deceive you.
I am selfish. I beseech you, take.

SELF-PORTRAIT, WOOD BLOCK

DELIA WARE KEEFE, *Pull, Kick, Glide*, 2005

The artist has stopped and bends like
    a calm mother over a wooden plank.
        Her hands may not hold for the work of it

but if they do they make a nest
    from each curling twig the plow has birthed into air.
        Because it's all confession anyway.

Once we write it down, at least. Once we
    carve it into the fine wood made for carving,
        the thin shina plane like water the woman's hands

glide through, palm against palm in prayer
    to her own body. Her breasts, too, gliding in the water,
        becoming the buoyancy, an inky

well of the spirit. It's a blue ink that she will roll
    over like a thick squid on the wood,
        pressing it down into the grooves, into

crevices that make the hands, the two hands praying,
    the two hands open to hold the water.
        Women do this.

For each print you must roll the ink.
    Though my body does not hold a secret
        like the stain on rice paper, I am spun

in the water for what they can haul
out of me, my head dangling
from the side of the ship, a great mass on a great hook—

the real treasure's there, my men. Heave to.
No, for it's spring on land. We must not forget
how the mud will turn forth its own green sea,

the wavering grass in the wind in a meadow
with the birds chirping dawn of a new spring.
The artist will turn to ink the nest in delicate pastels.

Don't be afraid. You have seen the colors change
like the sky before a storm. You have seen
the change and you are not afraid. Isn't it the same sky,

one you sang to as a girl with the ocean grass
like duned wings? It was the only safe place,
certainly it must have been, that deck

floating on aquatint. The rocks just below.
When you broke your finger catching
your own fall the neighbor offered to carry you

up from the jetty, but he had not seen you,
how you could make the world smaller
and smaller. World of the sea snail.

Infinite sand. All of it stone one day not today.
    Really the artist must think of a water
        calmer than this. We swam

in Scargo when even the Bay was too cold.
    She thinks of water too deep for measuring,
        a glacial surface making an electric skin into which

the pull and kick slice down and enter as ancient swords
    into the thick hide of a beast. Entering
        as soundings in the deep earth.

It was love that I sang about, as a girl, of course,
    love living in some prince. He would walk
        from the water (my song called to him)

and shake the seaweed from his shoulders.
    But we never met. I sang. I saw
        him. I sang. I never saw him. It was the voice then,

clashing in the sea air. Looking
    for the thing outside, something to balance
        against the waves, the artist prints her own body.

Smaller, younger, it floats as it stands,
    its edges marked by the seeping ink.

THE LITHOPEDION APOLOGIZES

In every family there's an aggressor.
Like the black-backed gull I feel you watch,
a salty warrior whose gapped mouth tells it ugly:
even you can see he's spent his life fighting.

So, he's become a freak—a chunk of his
beak missing and the rest grown up about
the hole in a tumorous calcium bulk.
The odd tongue showing through. It flicks pink.

Today could be October, this air,
but beauty is the sea's strength in June
and so, this morning we walked to Chapin
forgetting how we'd get back—then

pushed our way home against the wind.
Moisture changes every object's texture to skin.

Now the afternoon is only for gulls and kites,
coasting the air's chop, catching

themselves in the flock as they fall. All summer,
though you carry me long past due,
I've fought you, body, mother.

Wingless sheathed lithokelyphos, gull-child,
I've begun to admit it to myself:
I am her greatest failure.

Lulled by your walk, I dream of being cut free—
the harelip wound marking me wrong,
unhidden, open mouthed, eager for the squawk.

THE WOMEN CHANT WORDS
THAT CROSS LIKE TIDES

The women chant words that cross like tides.
Filaments become their hands, and extend

like the fingers that comb the netting down.
The fingers plait hair, a weaver's daughter

become mother and cradling her own head
back and forth. The weft moves under warp.

Over generations. Under generations because
the words cross and tangle in the women.

Each weft is a story chanted by the tides.
Upon words, the thread builds a woolen myth

and teems in the soft mechanism of the loom.
The women's hands cross like tides to stretch

the finally spun breath between them and
across the horizon. The words are the names

of born children. The tides cross, the hands
hold high the delicate plexus then, one swift cut.

A NOTE ON THE TYPE

Farnham is a refinement of the typefaces created by German-born punchcutter Johann Fleischman, a contemporary of Baskerville and Fournier, who worked at the Enschede Foundry in Haarlem. In the mid- to late 1700s, his letterforms and ornaments received wide acclaim across Europe for their angularity, energy, and "sparkle." Fleischman's work saw several digital revivals in the late twentieth century before its ultimate release as Farnham by type designer Christian Schwartz in 2004.